W9-AUI-607

Real Science-4-Kids

Biology

Level I

Rebecca W. Keller, Ph.D.

Cover design: David Keller
Opening page: David Keller
Illustrations: Rebecca W. Keller, Ph.D.

Real Science-4-Kids: Biology Level I Textbook

ISBN # 978-0974914923

Published by Gravitas Publications, Inc.
4116 Jackie Road SE, Suite 101
Rio Rancho, NM 87124
www.gravitaspublications.com

Special thanks to Susan Searles for copyediting and review of the manuscript. Also, I'd like to thank the Keller kids (Kimberly, Chris, and Katy), the Chesebrough kids (Sam and Ben), and the Megill kids (Lorien, Lee, Joshua, and Joseph) for critical evaluation of the text. Finally, I'd like to thank Lillian McLean for valuable input.

Printed in United States

Gravitas
Publications Inc.

Contents

Chapter 1 Living Creatures

1.1 The science of life

What is biology? The word biology comes from the Greek words *bios*, which means "life," and *logos*, which means "description." So biology is the field of science that "describes life." Biology is concerned with all living creatures and how they interact with one another.

Living creatures come in different sizes, shapes, and colors. Some are big and some are very small. Some are green, some are red, some are black, and some are white. Some see with two eyes, some see with eight eyes, and some have no eyes at all! Some fly, some walk, some swim, and some crawl.

Trees

Frogs

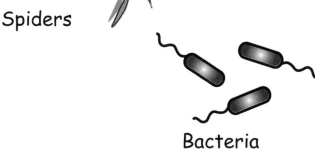

Spiders

Bacteria

There are many different kinds of living things but they all have one thing in common. They are all alive.

Both living creatures and nonliving things are made of the same material: atoms! But living creatures differ from nonliving things, like rocks and lakes and air, because they are living.

Living things require food to stay alive; they reproduce (have babies); some move freely in their environment; and eventually, all living things die. Living creatures are "alive" and nonliving things are not.

1.2 Taxonomy

One way to understand living things is to organize or classify them. By organizing the different types of living things, scientists can better study both their similarities and their differences.

The branch of biology concerned with naming and classifying the many different types of living things is called taxonomy (tak-sä'-nə-mē). Carolus Linnaeus (li-nē'-əs) (1707-1778), a Swedish physician, was the founder of taxonomy. Linnaeus viewed science as a way to understand how the world was organized. He began to carefully study all the living things he could find. Whenever he found animals that were similar, like dogs and wolves or bees and wasps, he grouped them together. Grouping things together is what is meant by classifying. A new creature is classified in a group depending on which creatures it looks like. Sometimes it is very hard to decide which group a creature fits into.

1.3 The kingdoms

Plantae
(plants)

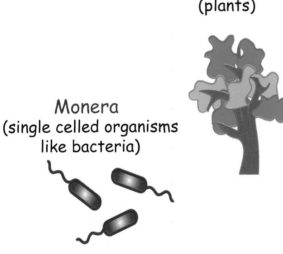

Monera
(single celled organisms
like bacteria)

Animalia
(animals)

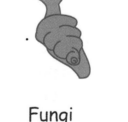

Protista
(single and multicellular organisms
like algae and paramecia)

Fungi
(including mushrooms)

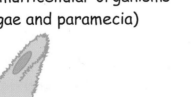

Because there are so many different kinds of living creatures, it has been hard for scientists to figure out exactly how to organize them. Several different approaches are currently in use. The most commonly used approach first divides all living things into five kingdoms. The kingdoms divide the various kinds of life into their largest groupings. The names of the kingdoms are Monera, Protista, Plantae, Fungi, and Animalia.

How do we decide which kingdom a living thing should be placed in?

Should a dog be grouped with the tigers, or should it be placed with the bacteria? Should a house cat be grouped with the house plants or with the bunnies? What about a snake? Is it like a mushroom or like a jellyfish?

There are several things that need to be considered when placing a living thing into a particular kingdom. However, it is mostly the difference in the structure of the cells that ultimately determines the kingdom in which an organism will be placed. Cells are the basic building blocks from which all life is made. We will learn more about cells in Chapter 2. Dog cells are more like tiger cells than bacteria, so dogs are grouped with tigers. Cat cells are more like bunny cells than plant cells, so cats are grouped with bunnies. Snakes and jellyfish, although very different from each other, have similar cells, so snakes are grouped with jellyfish and not mushrooms.

The animal kingdom, Animalia (ä-nə-māl'-yə), includes ALL of the animals: dogs, cats, frogs, sea urchins, bees, birds, snakes, jellyfish, bunnies, and even us! The animal kingdom has a wide variety of living creatures in it. Some are similar to each other, like dogs and wolves, and some are not so similar, like bees and snails, but ALL animals have animal cells. (See Chapter 2.) This distinguishes them from other living things.

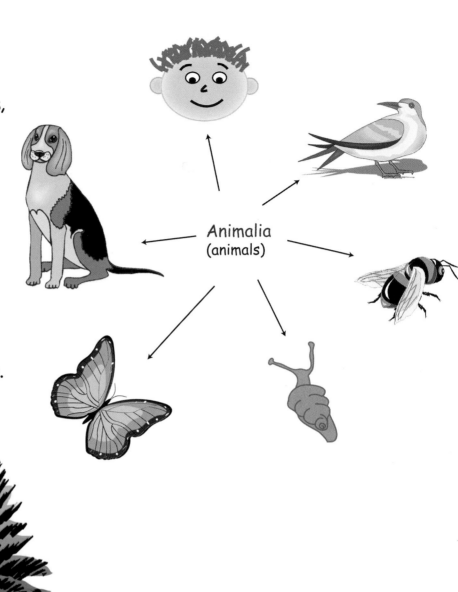

Animalia (animals)

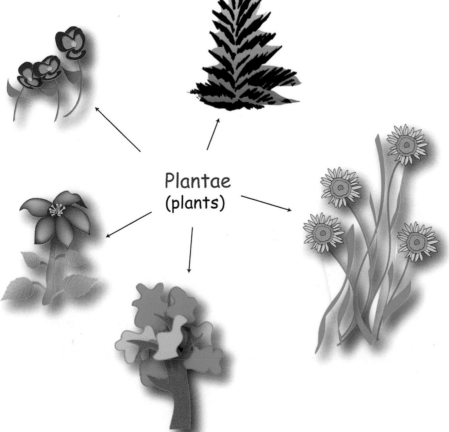

Plantae (plants)

The plant kingdom, Plantae, (plan'-tī) includes all plants: trees, grass, flowers, ferns, dandelions, seaweed, and even asparagus! Again, some plants are similar to each other and some plants are very, very different from each other, but ALL plants have plant cells. (See Chapter 2.)

The fungus kingdom, Fungi (fun'-jī) includes mushrooms, toadstools, truffles, and even athlete's foot! The fungi were once grouped as plants, but they have many unique features and are now placed in a kingdom of their own.

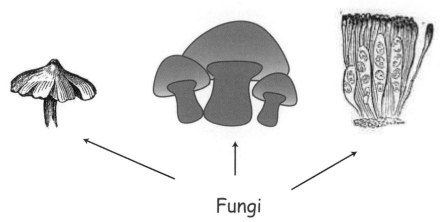

Fungi

The last two kingdoms, Protista (prō-tē'-stə) and Monera (mə-nē'-rə), include most of the microscopic organisms like bacteria and amoebas. These organisms cannot be seen with the unaided eye and were completely unknown before microscopes were invented.

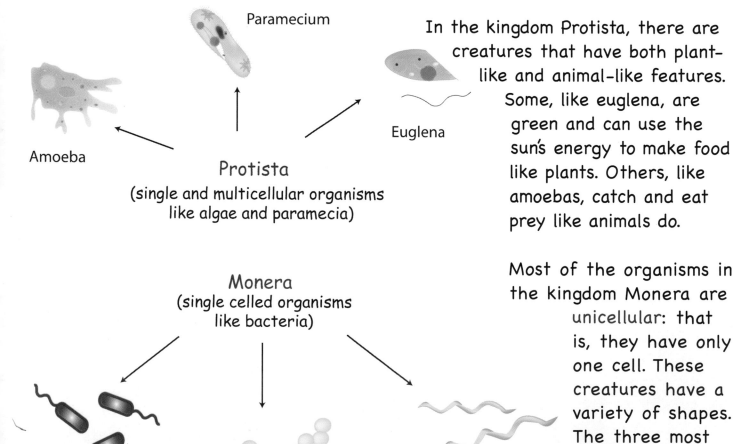

Paramecium

Amoeba

Protista
(single and multicellular organisms like algae and paramecia)

Euglena

In the kingdom Protista, there are creatures that have both plant-like and animal-like features. Some, like euglena, are green and can use the sun's energy to make food like plants. Others, like amoebas, catch and eat prey like animals do.

Monera
(single celled organisms like bacteria)

Most of the organisms in the kingdom Monera are unicellular: that is, they have only one cell. These creatures have a variety of shapes. The three most common shapes are spheres, rods and spirals.

Rods

Spheres

Sprirals

1.4 Further classification

Once a living thing has been placed into a kingdom, the classification continues. Living things are further organized by being placed in additional categories that depend on a variety of criteria, like whether or not they have a backbone or whether or not they lay eggs. For example, although all animals are in the kingdom Animalia, it seems obvious that dogs and bees and snakes should be in different groups.

Kingdom - Animalia

Phylum - Arthropoda

Phylum - Chordata

Class - Amphibia

Class - Mammalia

Order - Carnivora

Family - Felidae

Family - Canidae

Kingdoms are divided into smaller groups called phyla (fī'-lə). Dogs, frogs, and cats are members of the phylum Chordata (kȯr-dā'-tə) because they all have backbones, and bees are in the phylum Arthropoda (är-thrə-pō'-də) because they have "jointed feet." In the same way, the phyla are divided into smaller groups called classes. Dogs and cats are all in the class Mammalia (mə-māl'-yə) because they nurse their young, and frogs are in the class Amphibia (am-fi'-bē-ə) because they live both in water and on land. Classes are further divided into orders. Both cats and dogs are in the order Carnivora (kär-ni'-və-rə) because they eat meat. Orders are further divided into families. Cats are in the family Felidae (fē'-lə-dī), and dogs are in the family Canidae (kan'-ə-dī).

1.5 Naming living things

Finally, families are further divided into the genus (jē'-nəs), and the genus is divided into the species (spē'-shēz). The genus is the last group in which a living creature is placed, and the species identifies each creature placed in the genus, so each different living thing has a unique genus and species name. For example both a bobcat and a house cat are in the genus *Felis* (fē'-lis). A bobcat has the species name *rufa* (roo'-fə) and a house cat has the species name *catus* (ca'-tus). So a house cat is a *Felis catus* and a bobcat is a *Felis rufa*.

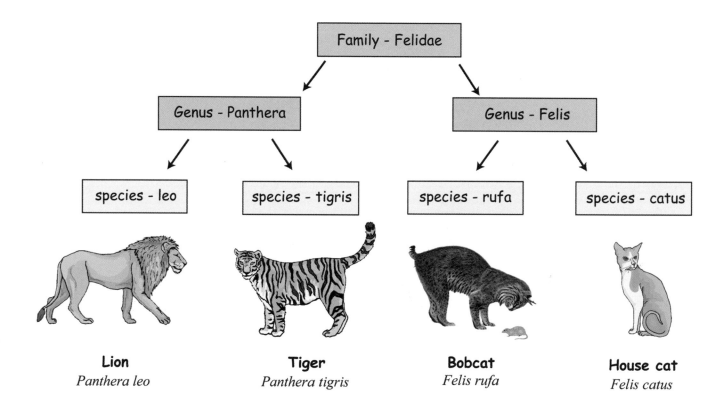

| Lion | Tiger | Bobcat | House cat |
| *Panthera leo* | *Panthera tigris* | *Felis rufa* | *Felis catus* |

A tiger is a kind of cat, but it is different from both bobcats and house cats. It is in the genus *Panthera* (pan-thē'-rə) and has a species name *tigris* (tī'-gris). So, a tiger is called a *Panthera tigris*. A lion is like a tiger and is also in the genus *Panthera*, but it has a species name *leo* (lē'-ō), so it is a *Panthera leo*.

All living things have a particular genus and species name. The name for household dogs is *Canis familiaris* (ka'-nis fə-mil-ē-ā'-ris), and for humans it is *Homo sapiens* (hō'-mō sā'-pē-enz), which means "man wise."

1.6 Summary

Here are the main points to remember from this chapter:

° Biology is the study of living things. Taxonomy is a branch of biology that classifies living things.

° All living things are classified into different groups. The largest group is the kingdom. The five kingdoms are divided into phylum, then class, order, family, genus and species. Living things are placed in a group depending on many characteristics, including what kind of cells they have, whether they have hair or scales, and whether or not they lay eggs.

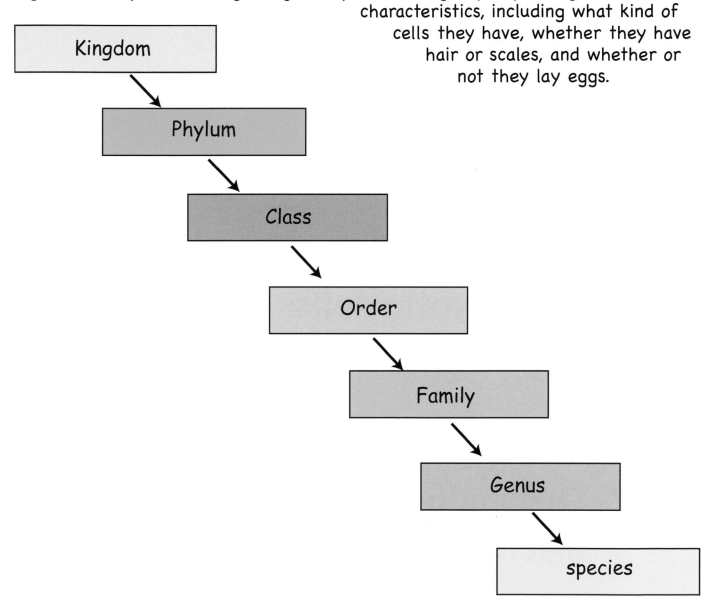

° Living things are grouped into these categories so that scientists can learn more about how they are the same and how they are different. Also, if a new creature is discovered, say from the deep ocean floor, it can be placed into a group that will help scientists identify it and better understand how it lives.

Chapter 2 Cells—The Building Blocks of Life

2.1 Introduction

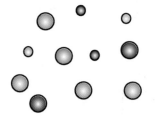

Atoms

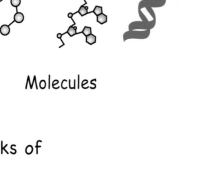

Molecules

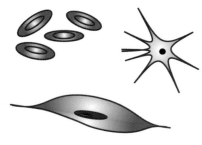

Cells

All living things are made of a complex and highly ordered arrangement of atoms and molecules that fit together to form cells. Cells are the building blocks of all living things.

Amoeba

Paramecium

The smallest living things have only a single cell, like amoebas and paramecia. These single-celled creatures live alone or in colonies. They do many of the same things that bigger creatures do, but with a single cell. However, bigger creatures, like people and ponies, are made of many cells. In these creatures, the cells fit together to form tissues.

Tissues are made of many cells, and each tissue has its own job. For example, muscles are made of muscle tissue, and skin is made of skin tissue. Skin and muscles are called organs.

Tissues

Organism

Organs each have their own job to do and cannot swap jobs. For example, eyes are used for seeing and ears are used for hearing. Think how hard it would be to see with your ears or hear with your eyes! Organs, in turn, fit together to form an organism—or living creature. Both large creatures and small creatures have many organs. Some organs from different creatures are similar, but each organ is made for a particular organism. All of the organs work together so that the living creature can eat, reproduce, move or stay in one place, and live.

The cell — a small factory

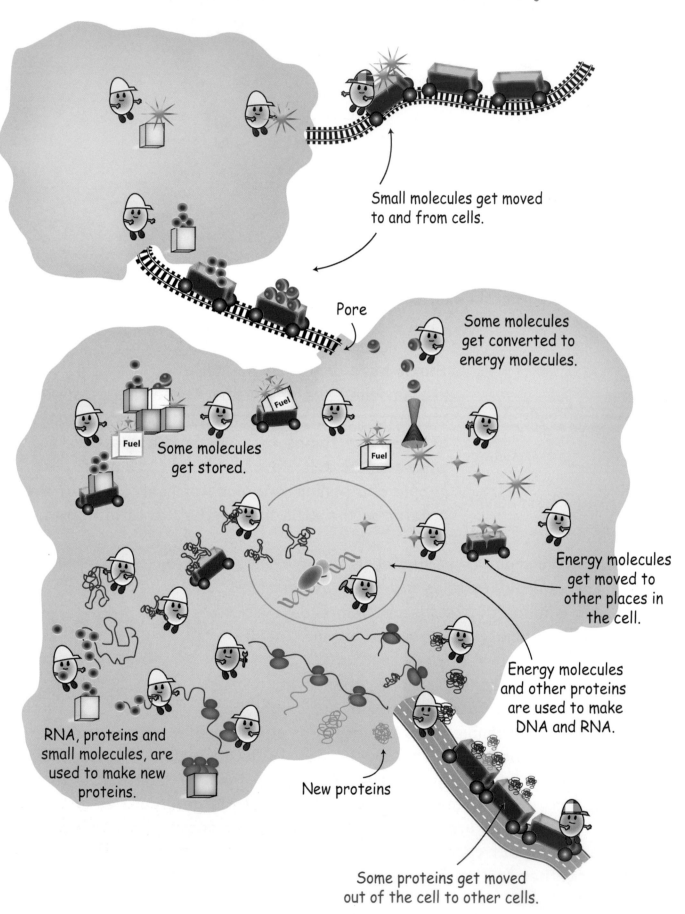

Small molecules get moved to and from cells.

Pore

Some molecules get converted to energy molecules.

Some molecules get stored.

Fuel

Energy molecules get moved to other places in the cell.

Energy molecules and other proteins are used to make DNA and RNA.

RNA, proteins and small molecules, are used to make new proteins.

New proteins

Some proteins get moved out of the cell to other cells.

2.2 The cell — a small factory

Each cell is like a little factory. All of the molecules in the cell have special jobs to do. There are many different kinds of molecules inside cells. Most of the big molecules are proteins (prō'-tēnz), but there are also sugars and nucleic (nü-klā'-ik) acids. Small molecules, like water and salt, are also in cells.

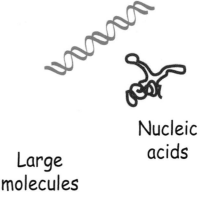

Nucleic
acids

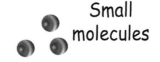

Large
molecules

Small
molecules

The proteins in the cell are like tiny machines. They do most of the work. For example, proteins move other proteins and small molecules in and out of the cell. Proteins make other proteins and nucleic acids, such as DNA. Proteins also take small molecules and make large molecules. For example, they use sugar molecules to make carbohydrates.

Proteins

The inside of the cell is highly organized. The proteins and DNA cannot be just anywhere in the cell, but must work in particular places. For example, the proteins that are used to take molecules in and out of the cell are found near special places called pores. Pores are like little tunnels that go through the walls of the cell. Molecules can move in and out through them.

The cell "knows" where all of the molecules are and how many proteins are working. This way the cell always has just the right number of proteins working in a particular area so that there are not too many proteins making DNA and too few making carbohydrates.

The proteins and other molecules in the cell never rest. They are always working. If they stop working, the cell can no longer live. When cells get old or damaged, the proteins and other molecules cannot work, and the cell dies. Eventually, all cells in all living things die. When a cell dies, all of the parts of the cell break down into smaller molecules. All of the molecules from dead cells are used again to make new molecules for a different cell.

2.3 Types of cells

There are two major types of cells. They are called prokaryotic (prō-ka-rē-ä'-tik) cells and eukaryotic (yü-ka-rē-ä'-tik) cells.

Prokaryote (prō-ka'-rē-ōt) comes from the Greek words *pro*, which means "before" and *karyon* which means "kernel." So prokaryote means "before kernel." This term refers to the fact that prokaryotes *do not* have a nucleus. A nucleus (nü'-klē-əs) is a small "sack" inside the cell that holds the DNA.

Eukaryotes *do* have a nucleus. Eukaryote (yü-ka'-rē-ōt) comes from the Greek words *eu,* meaning "true," and *karyon*, meaning "kernel." Eukaryote means "true kernel," which describes the fact that a eukaryote has a nucleus. Eukaryotic cells are usually much bigger and more complex than prokaryotic cells.

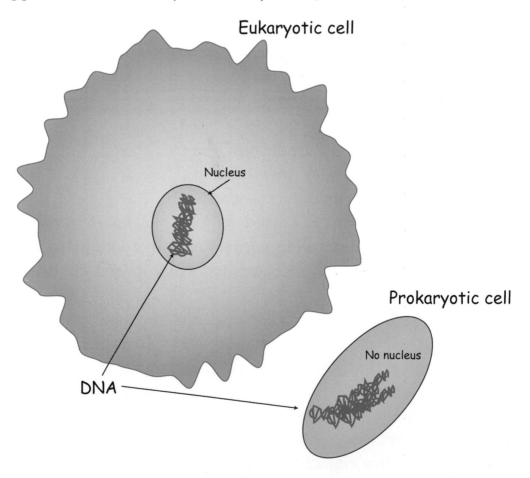

All bacteria (kingdom Monera) are prokaryotes, and all other living things, like plants and animals (kingdoms Plantae, Animalia, Fungi, and Protista) are eukaryotes. (See Sections 2.5 and 2.6)

2.4 Prokaryotic cells

The simplest cells are the prokaryotic cells. Recall that prokaryotes do not have a nucleus. Instead, the DNA is kept in a region called the nucleoid (nü'-klē-oid). This is a central region in the cell that is not physically separated from the rest of the cell by a membrane. Prokaryotic cells are surrounded by a cell wall and a plasma membrane.

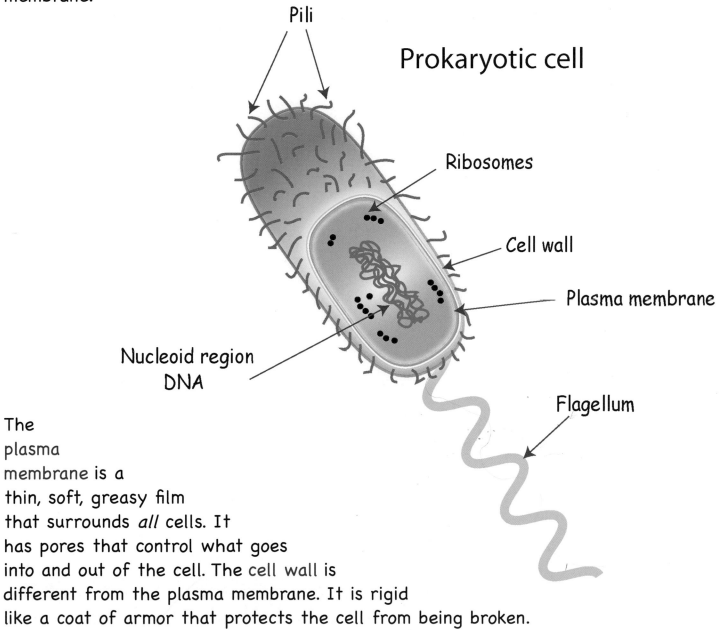

Pili

Prokaryotic cell

Ribosomes

Cell wall

Plasma membrane

Nucleoid region
DNA

Flagellum

The plasma membrane is a thin, soft, greasy film that surrounds *all* cells. It has pores that control what goes into and out of the cell. The cell wall is different from the plasma membrane. It is rigid like a coat of armor that protects the cell from being broken.

Many prokaryotic cells have flagella (flə-je'-lə). These are long or short "whips" that help the cell move around. A flagellum is connected to a complicated motor that twirls around with great speed and propels the cell in all directions. Some prokaryotes also have pili (pī'-lī). Pili are long "threads" that help the cell stick to surfaces and other cells.

2.5 Plant cells

Plant cells are eukaryotic cells. Plants are eukaryotes because they have a nucleus that holds the DNA and other machinery required to copy and use the DNA. The nucleus is a type of organelle (ôr-gə-nel').

Only eukaryotic cells have organelles; prokaryotic cells do not. Organelles function as little organs inside a cell. They are not true organs because true organs are made up of many cells, but they can be considered little organs inside cells. Another example of an organelle is the chloroplast (klôr'-ə-plast). Plants use chloroplasts to convert the sun's energy into food. (See Chapter 3.)

Mitochondrion

Microtubules

Central vacuole

Nucleus

Nucleolus

Ribosomes

Rough endoplasmic reticulum

Chloropla

Peroxisomes

Plasma membrane

Cell wall

Golgi apparatus

When cells were first observed, microscopes were not very powerful. Scientists thought cells were simple sacks because they couldn't see the organelles and other cell parts. Today, scientists know that cells are not simple at all, but contain complex machinery that is highly organized. Many of the cell's functions are performed by organelles. There are also machines inside cells which perform specific tasks but are not organelles. For example, ribosomes (rī'-bə-sōmz) are machines that make proteins. Machines like ribosomes are found in both prokaryotic and eukaryotic cells.

2.6 Animal cells

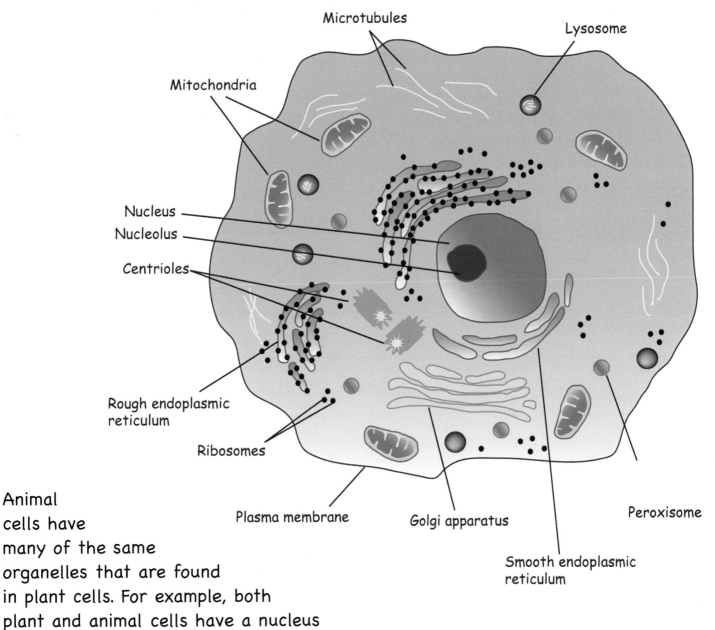

Microtubules

Lysosome

Mitochondria

Nucleus

Nucleolus

Centrioles

Rough endoplasmic
reticulum

Ribosomes

Plasma membrane

Golgi apparatus

Peroxisome

Smooth endoplasmic
reticulum

Animal cells have many of the same organelles that are found in plant cells. For example, both plant and animal cells have a nucleus to hold the DNA, and both have mitochondria (mī-tə-kän'-drē-ə) which are small factories that make energy molecules. Both plant and animal cells have a rough endoplasmic reticulum (en-də-plaz'-mik ri-ti'-kyə-ləm) where proteins are made, and both have microtubules (mī-krō-tü'-byülz) that are used to move things from place to place in the cell.

But animal cells *do not* have a cell wall. Instead, they are surrounded only by the plasma membrane. Also, animal cells do not have chloroplasts like plant cells and cannot make their own food with sunlight. So, although plant and animal cells have many similar features, they also have important differences.

2.7 Organelles and cell machinery

The following is a partial list of some organelles and other cell machinery.

Nucleus
(organelle)

The nucleus is the central part of the cell. It holds all of the information the cell needs to live and reproduce.

Nucleolus
(organelle)

The place where pieces of ribosomes are made.

Mitochondria
(organelle)

This is where the cell's energy molecules are made.

Rough endoplasmic reticulum
(organelle)

The place where proteins and new membranes are made.

ribosomes

Ribosomes
(molecular machine)

Ribosomes make proteins.

Peroxisomes
(organelle)

This is where the cell gets rid of dangerous and poisonous substances.

Lysosome
(organelle)

The place in the cell where some big molecules get digested for other uses by the cell.

Golgi apparatus
(organelle)

This is the shipping and receiving part of the cell. Proteins are modified and shipped or stored here.

Chloroplast (plants)
(organelle)

Uses light energy from the sun to make energy molecules for the cell.

Cell wall
(plants, prokaryotes)
(organelle)

Because plants have no skeleton, the cell wall is rigid to help plants hold their shape.

2.8 Summary

Here are the main points to remember from this chapter:

○ All living things are made of cells.

○ Cells are very complex and function like small factories.

○ There are two basic types of cells: prokaryotic cells and eukaryotic cells.

○ Only eukaryotic cells have organelles inside their cells.

○ In multi-cellular organisms, many cells fit together to form tissues. The tissues fit together to make organs, and the organs work together in the organism.

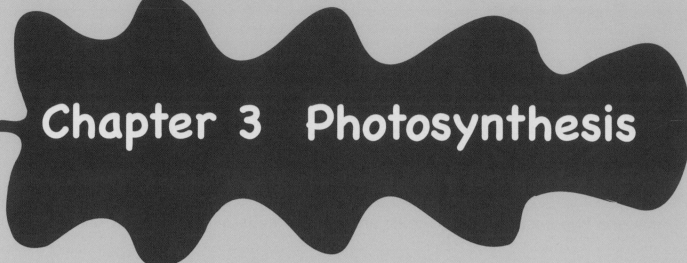

Chapter 3   Photosynthesis

3.1 Introduction

Why can't plants eat cheeseburgers? If they can't eat cheeseburgers, how do they get their food?

Although a few plants do eat small insects (but never cheeseburgers), most plants use the sun's energy to *make* food. Plants make their food by a process called photosynthesis (fō-tō-sin'-thə-səs). Photo comes from the Greek word *photos* which means "light," and *synthesis* means "to make," so photosynthesis means "to make with light." Plants use the energy from the sun's light to make their own food. They do this with organelles inside their cells.

3.2 Chloroplasts

Plants have special organelles in their cells that allow them to use the sun's light to make food. These organelles are called chloroplasts. Chloroplasts capture the sun's energy and make sugars from carbon dioxide (dī-äk'-sīd) and water. The molecule that captures the sun's energy is chlorophyll (klôr'-ə-fil) which gives plants a green color.

It takes energy to make sugar—light from the sun is a form of energy. When light hits a plant cell, the energy is absorbed by chlorophyll molecules. The chlorophyll molecules are very carefully organized inside the chloroplast in an area called the thylakoid (thī'-lə-koid). The chlorophyll molecules give the energy they get from the sun to a series of protein machines that make sugar molecules. The plant then uses the sugar molecules for food. Plants *use* carbon dioxide, CO_2, to make their food, and they *release* oxygen (äk'-si-jən), O_2, into the air.

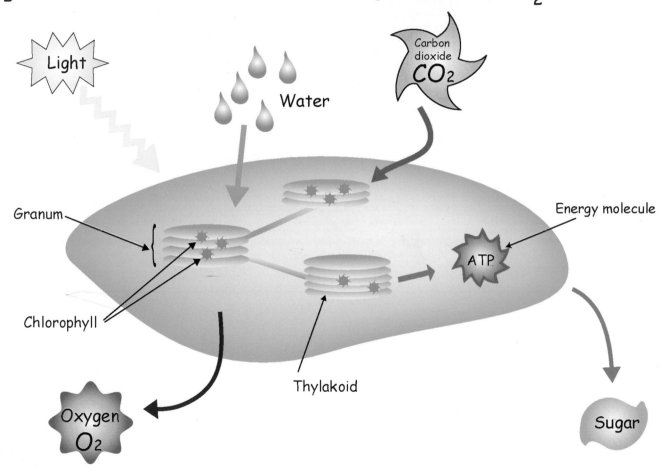

All of the green parts of a plant have chloroplasts and chlorophyll. The unripened fruit of a plant also contains chloroplasts, but the leaves of the plant contain the most. Leaves are the primary organ of the plant that conducts photosynthesis.

3.3 Why plants have leaves

Because of their design, leaves can collect much more sunlight than any other part of the plant. The leaves of flowering plants usually have a broad, flat shape. This shape enables them to collect as much sunlight as possible.

On a tree, the leaves are fixed to the branches at many different angles. This helps the leaves collect sunlight in all directions during the day, even as the sun moves in the sky.

Many evergreen trees have needles instead of broad, flat leaves. Needles are very narrow leaves with a thick outer coating. Trees that have needles are uniquely designed to live in places where it is drier and where broad, flat leaves would tend to dry out.

In the winter a small amount of photosynthesis occurs, which is why evergreen needles remain green throughout the year. This is why they are called evergreen. Evergreen trees that have needles are also called conifers (kä'-nə-fərz) because they have cones. Conifer comes from the Latin word *conus* which means "cone" and *ferre* which means "to carry." So a conifer is a tree that "carries cones."

3.4 Photosynthesis in other organisms

Some organisms that are not classified as plants also use the sun's energy to make food. For example, many types of algae (al'-jē) are photosynthetic. Algae can be microscopic (that is, they cannot be seen without the aid of a microscope) and macroscopic (large enough to see with our eyes alone). The seaweeds found in the ocean are classified as algae rather than true plants. Seaweeds may look like water plants, but they are not true plants because they lack many features common to land plants, like roots, stems, and leaves.

Not all seaweeds are green. Some are red or brown. However, seaweeds do use photosynthesis to make their own food, just like land plants do. In fact, microscopic algae make most of the food for the animals in the ocean!

Another class of organism that uses the sun's energy to make food is the cyanobacteria (sī-an-ō-bak-tir'-rē-ə). Cyanobacteria were once called blue-green algae, but because they don't have a nucleus (they are prokaryotes), they are not like other algae. They are now grouped with the bacteria.

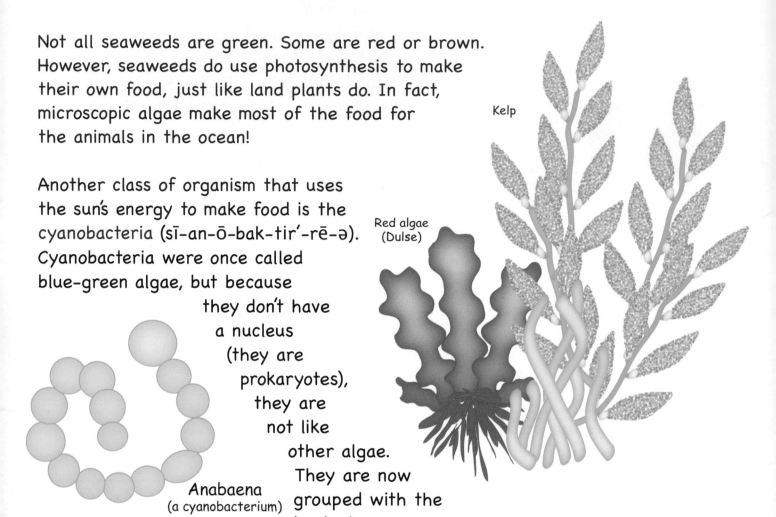

Kelp

Red algae (Dulse)

Anabaena
(a cyanobacterium)

3.5 Summary

Here are the main points to remember from this chapter:

° Plants use the sun's energy to make food.

° Using the sun's energy to make food is called photosynthesis.

° Chloroplasts are organelles inside plant cells that are responsible for photosynthesis.

° All of the green parts of a plant have chloroplasts, but leaves do most of the photosynthesis.

Chapter 4 Parts of a Plant

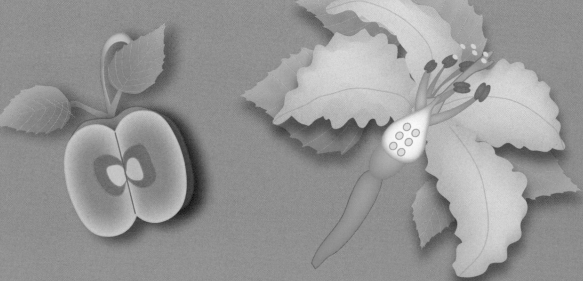

4.1 Introduction

Plants ultimately provide food for all creatures that inhabit the world. Plants are eaten by many animals that are, in turn, eaten by us!

Cows, pigs, and sheep all eat plants. Plants also make the oxygen that we breathe. It would take several thousand years, but without plants eventually we would not have enough oxygen to survive.

There are more than 250,000 different types of known plants. Plants range in size from the very tiny wildflower that grows on the forest floor, to the giant redwoods in California. Plants also vary in color and design. Some plants grow beautiful flowers that look lovely in a garden, and some plants have spikes all over them that are prickly to touch.

4.2 How plants live

Plants are uniquely designed to live in the Earth's soil. Plants must be able to take in nutrients from both the soil and the air above the soil.

To accomplish this task, plants have different parts that perform different functions. The three main parts of plants are the roots, stems, and leaves. Flowering plants have a fourth part, the flowers. Some parts of the plant are in the soil, like the roots. Other parts are in the air above the soil, like the stems, leaves, and flowers. Because plants have parts in both the soil and in the air above the soil, they can take in nutrients from both places.

Flower

Stem

Leaves

Roots

These different parts are called organs because they are made of many tissues and each has a special job to perform, just like the organs in our own bodies.

The organs of a plant cannot live on their own, but they can work together to make the whole plant. If a flower is cut from the stem of a living plant, the flower soon withers and dies. If a stem is cut from the roots of the plant, it will not survive. Plants need all of their organs to live, just like we do!

4.3 Parts of a plant: roots

The part of the plant that lives below the soil is called the root system. The roots serve two functions. First, they are required to firmly anchor the plant in the soil to prevent strong winds and rains from pulling the plant out. Second, the roots provide water and minerals needed for making food.

There are two different kinds of roots. Some plants have a central root, called a taproot, that extends very deep into the soil.

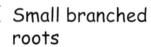

Small branched roots

Taproot

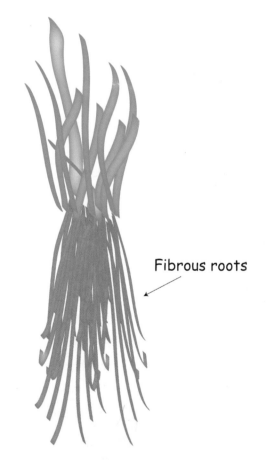

Fibrous roots

Smaller roots branch from the taproot in all directions. A dandelion has this type of root system.

Grass roots, on the other hand, are long, thin strings with no taproot. These are called fibrous (fī'-brus) roots because they look like fibers. Fibrous roots provide excellent stability for the plant. Grasses are not easily pulled out by rain and wind.

All root tissues are designed to take in water and minerals from the soil. The roots move the water and minerals to the upper part of the plant where the food is made.

4.4 Parts of a plant: stems

The food a plant makes by photosynthesis is made in the upper portion of the plant which is called the shoot system. The shoot system includes the leaves of the plant, the stem, and also the flowers and fruit of the plant. The shoot system contains the *photosynthetic machinery* needed for making food. Remember that photosynthesis occurs in the chloroplasts that are found in all of the green parts of the plant. Once the food is made, it is transported (moved) to other parts of the shoot system, such as flowers and fruit, and also down to the roots.

Two special types of tissues are used to move the food, water, and minerals to various parts of the plant. These tissues are called the xylem (zī'-ləm) and the phloem (flō'-əm). In many plants, the xylem and phloem surround a central core of tissues called the pith. The pith stores food and water for the plant.

The xylem transports minerals and water in an upward direction, beginning from the roots, to the stem system of the plant. The phloem brings food (made through photosynthesis) downward from the leaves to the lower parts of the plant. The phloem surrounds the xylem and is the main tissue found in the bark or outer part of the stem.

Both the xylem and the phloem are required for the plant to grow and remain healthy.

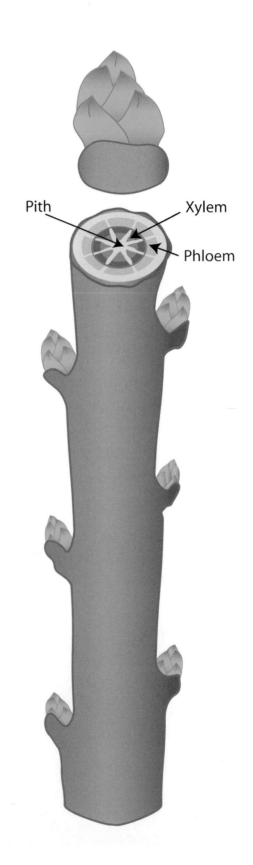

Pith   Xylem   Phloem

4.5 Parts of a plant: flowers

In many plants, flowers are used to make new plants. Flowers provide the plant with the means to reproduce or make new plants.

The colorful petals of a flower help attract bees and other insects. The bees pick up pollen on their legs and take it from plant to plant. Pollen is needed by the flower to form a new plant. Pollen grains are produced at the ends of the stamens (stā'-mənz) and collected at the end of a tall stem called the carpel (kar'-pəl). Once inside the carpel, the pollen travels down to the ovary, where an egg is located. The pollen causes changes in the egg that cause the flower to turn into a fruit.

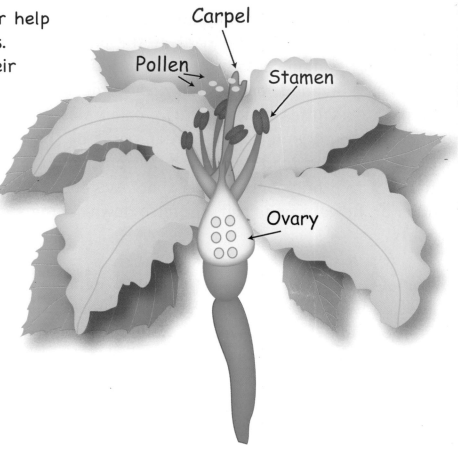

Once the egg and the pollen combine, the flower dies and a fruit develops. The fruit holds the egg and pollen that have now turned into a seed. If the seed finds the right conditions, it can grow into a new plant. This is one way that plants reproduce to make more plants.

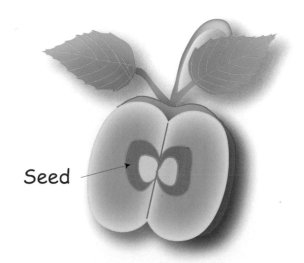

4.6 Summary

Here are the most important points to remember from this chapter:

○ Plants ultimately provide food for all living things. Without plants we could not live.

○ Plants are designed to live in both the Earth's soil and in air. They have three main parts: the roots, the stems, and the leaves. Flowering plants also have flowers. All of these are called organs.

○ The roots provide the plant with nutrients from the soil and serve as an anchor.

○ The stems have tissues that move nutrients from the leaves to the roots (phloem), and tissues that move water and nutrients from the roots to the leaves (xylem).

○ The leaves use the sun's light to make food for the plant.

○ The flowers on flowering plants are involved in making new plants.

Chapter 5 How a Plant Grows

5.1 Introduction

As we saw in the last chapter, some plants are small, like a dandelion or a violet, and some plants are very big, like the giant redwoods of northern California. However, all flowering plants, big and small, start life as tiny seeds.

5.2 Flowers, fruits, and seeds

Flowers

As we saw in Chapter 4, the fruit is formed by the flower, and every flowering plant has some kind of flower. We call roses and violets "flowers" because they are especially big and beautiful. Apple trees and cherry trees have smaller flowers which turn into tasty fruit. Even pine trees have flowers: we call them pine cones.

Tree blossoms

Colorful flowers

Pine cone

Fruits and seeds

Sweet fruit of a cherry tree

Seeds are found in the fruit of every flowering plant. Fruits come in all different shapes, sizes, and flavors. Some fruits are sweet, like oranges and cherries. Some fruits are not sweet at all, like avocados and tomatoes. Some fruits can't be eaten. But all fruits contain seeds.

Maple fruit with "wings"

Apple seeds

Avocado seed

Every plant has its own kind of seed, and they all look a little different. Some seeds are small, like apple seeds; and some seeds are very large, like an avocado seed. Some seeds are housed in fruits with special features, like the "wings" on a maple seed that help it ride the wind to a new place before growing into a plant.

5.3 The seed

All seeds are basically "baby plants". Inside there is a tiny plant called an embryo (em´-brē-ō). This embryo will eventually grow into a mature plant. Seeds also have a big supply of stored food that helps the baby plant grow. The area where the food is stored is called the cotyledon (kä-tə-lē´-dən). The cotyledon makes up most of the space in the seed. The cotyledon and the embryo are inside a tough outer coating called the seed coat. The seed coat protects the embryo until the right conditions allow the seed to start growing.

Pinto bean seed

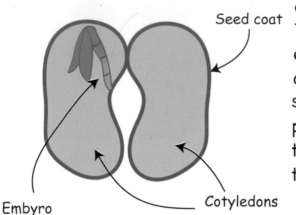

Seed coat

Embyro

Cotyledons

5.4 The seedling

When the conditions are right, the seed begins to grow into a young plant or seedling. This is called germination (jər-mə-nā´-shən). Germination begins when there is enough water to swell and break the outer seed coat. This is a signal for the embryo to start forming a plant. First, a root forms that pushes itself out from the side of the seed. The root enlarges until eventually a short stem emerges from the top of the seed. This stem forms a hook which helps push the new plant through the soil. Once the seed is out of the soil, sunlight stimulates the little plant to straighten out, lifting the cotyledons as new leaves emerge.

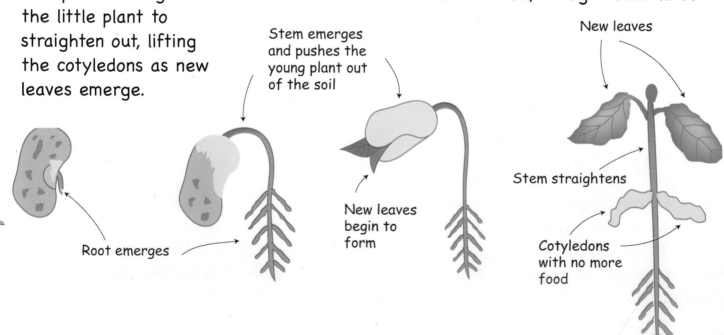

Root emerges

Stem emerges and pushes the young plant out of the soil

New leaves begin to form

New leaves

Stem straightens

Cotyledons with no more food

Inside the leaves, chloroplasts begin to form, turning the leaves green and producing food. At this point, the cotyledons are no longer needed and they wither and fall away from the seedling.

5.5 Signals for plant growth

How does a plant know which direction to grow in? If the seed is upside down in the soil, will the plant grow in the opposite direction?

There are different signals that plants use to tell which way to grow. A signal is like a traffic light or a road sign. Some signals tell the plant which way is up and which way is down. Other signals tell seeds when to start growing and when to wait. Still others tell plants when to lose leaves in the autumn and when to grow new ones in the spring.

For example, sunlight is a signal that tells the plant when it has broken the surface of the soil. The seedling needs to know when to stop growing the stem and begin growing the leaves. If a bean seedling is given water but no sunlight, it will grow a long stem with a hook at its tip, but the leaves will stay tiny and will not turn green. When the food reserves in the cotyledons are used up, this seedling stops growing and dies.

Gravity is also a signal to the young seedling. Gravity tells the plant in which direction it should extend the roots and in which direction to send the growing stem and new leaves. Special chemicals in the tissues of roots and stems help the plant determine which way is "up" and which way is "down." Gravity signals the plant so that the roots grow downward into the soil, and the leaves grow upward, where they can use the sun's energy to make food.

UP

STOP

EXIT HERE

DOWN

5.6 Plant nutrition

What things do plants need to have in order to grow? We already know that plants need the sun's light to make energy molecules, but are there other things that plants need in order to grow properly?

Most plants cannot grow in water alone. To fully develop, they require minerals. These minerals include the elements phosphorus (P), calcium (Ca), magnesium (Mg), nitrogen (N), potassium (K), zinc (Zn), iron (Fe), manganese (Mn), and sulfur (S). If a plant lacks any of these essential minerals, it does not necessarily die, but it may look sickly and not grow well. For example, if a plant lacks calcium (Ca), the young leaves will be yellow and crinkly. If the plant lacks nitrogen (N), the older leaves turn yellow and die prematurely. The plant will not grow to its full size; it is "stunted."

Growth is stunted

Leaves are yellow

Healthy plant   Plant without nitrogen

Plants get their minerals from the soil. The soil is actually a complex mixture of many different things. Soil contains living things like bacteria, fungi, earthworms, and insects. Soil also contains water and dissolved minerals. All of these things contribute to the growth and health of plants. For example, nitrogen (N) is required for healthy plant growth. Nitrogen is found in the air, but plants cannot use it directly. However, bacteria in the soil *can* convert nitrogen to a form that can be used by plants. Bacteria are often essential for helping plants grow.

5.7 The life cycle of flowering plants

In summary, the life cycle of a flowering plant begins with the formation of seeds inside the flower. The pollen prepares the eggs for reproduction, or fertilizes the eggs, which are in the ovary at the base of the flower. Once the egg is fertilized, a fruit develops and the flower withers away. When the fruit is ripe, it falls off the plant onto the ground. Because the fruit is no longer on the plant, it dies and releases its seeds onto the ground. If the conditions are right, the seed begins to grow into a new plant. Eventually, the new plant will grow new flowers that make new seeds. So the life cycle of the plant repeats.

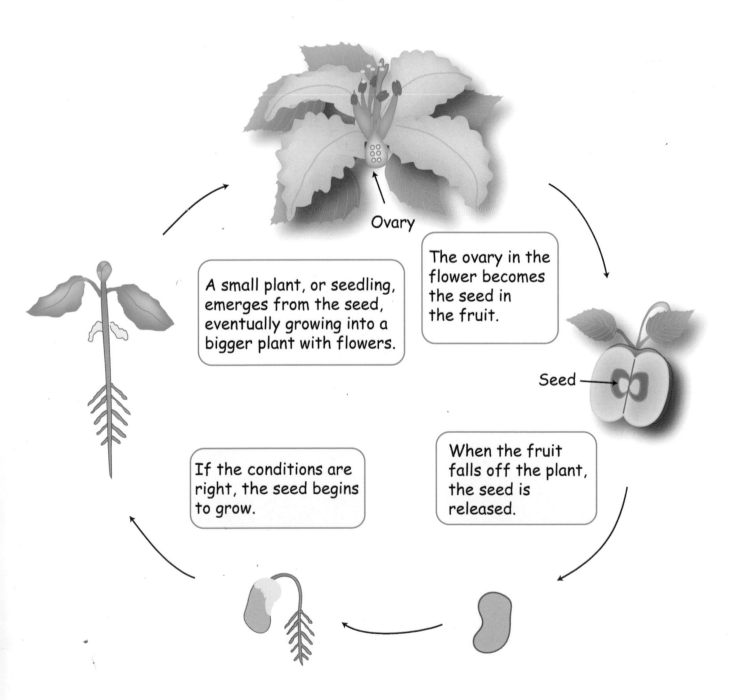

Ovary

A small plant, or seedling, emerges from the seed, eventually growing into a bigger plant with flowers.

The ovary in the flower becomes the seed in the fruit.

Seed

If the conditions are right, the seed begins to grow.

When the fruit falls off the plant, the seed is released.

5.8 Summary

Here are the most important things to remember from this chapter:

- All flowering plants begin life as seeds.

- Seeds come in many shapes and sizes and have a tiny plant inside them called an embryo.

- The embryo grows into a seedling and eventually into a mature plant.

- Plants have signals that tell them in which direction to grow. Gravity and sunlight are two such signals.

- Plants need minerals and other nutrients in order to grow properly.

Chapter 6 Protists I

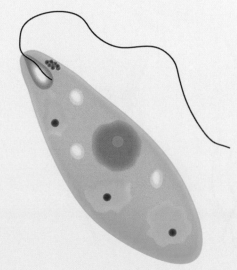

6.1 Introduction

Protists, also called protozoa (prō-tə-zō'-ə), are tiny creatures that are like both plants and animals. Most are made of only one cell. They are so small that they cannot be seen with the naked eye. For most of human history, nobody knew they even existed. However, in the middle of the 17th century, the first microscopes were invented and an entirely new world of microscopic organisms, including protists, was found. Protists live almost everywhere, including soil, freshwater ponds, and saltwater oceans.

Despite their small size, protists are amazing creatures. They crawl, swim, and divide in half. Some hunt for food like animals, and others can make their own food from sunlight using photosynthesis, just like plants. A few protists can even do both! Protists are some of the most elaborate and complex cells known to man.

(Euglena)

(Paramecium)

(Amoeba)

Various types of protists

6.2 The microscope

There are protists around us all of the time, but because they are single-celled organisms, they are not easily seen without a microscope.

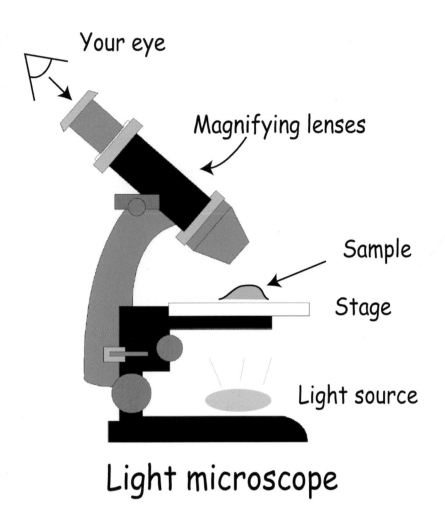

Your eye

Magnifying lenses

Sample

Stage

Light source

Light microscope

A microscope makes very small objects appear larger. Scientists use several different types of microscopes to look at cells, molecules, and even individual atoms! However, the easiest microscope to use, especially for students, is the *light* microscope. A light microscope is like a very powerful magnifying glass.

To use a light microscope, the sample is placed below the magnifying lenses, usually on a small platform called a stage. In modern microscopes, the sample is illuminated with a light source that is placed either above or below the sample. This extra light illuminates the small structures found in microscopic samples.

In 1665, Robert Hooke, an English scientist, was the first person to observe cells with a small microscope. He was able to magnify thin slices of cork 30 times (30X) and was able to see individual cork cells. Around the same time, Anton van Leeuwenhoek (lā'-vən-huk), a Dutchman, made a much more powerful microscope. He magnified pond water 300 times (300X) and saw tiny one-celled "animalcules" swimming around. He was the first person to observe the single-celled organisms that we now call protists. Much to his dismay, he even found protists living in his mouth!

6.3 Movement

There are almost 60,000 known species of protists. This is as many as the number of known plants and animals in the visible world. Although protists are classified in the single kingdom, Protista, they vary in structure and function more than any other group of organisms. Protists are divided into three main groups, depending mostly on how they move: the ciliates (si'-lē-āts), the flagellates (fla'-jə-lāts), and the amoeba (ə-mē'-bə).

Ciliates

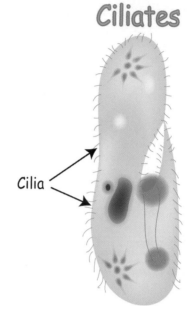

The ciliates swim with very small hair-like projections on their bodies called cilia (si'-lē-ə). The cilia beat very rapidly and propel the tiny creature through the water like a little submarine. A paramecium (pa-rə-mē'-sē-əm) is a type of ciliate.

Cilia

Paramecium

Flagellates

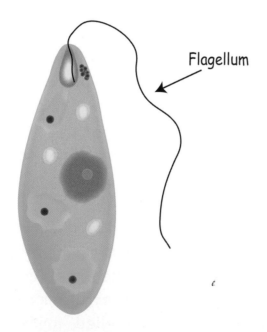

Flagellum

Euglena

Flagellates also swim, but instead of many short, hair-like projections, flagellates have only one or two long, whip-like flagella (flə-je'-lə) that extend from one end of their body. These whips propel the flagellate through the water much like the tail of a fish. A euglena (yoo-glē'-nə) is a type of flagellate.

Amoeba

Amoebas move very differently; they do not swim or use flagella or cilia. Instead, amoebas crawl along surfaces by extending and bulging the edges of their membranes. The portions of their membranes that stick out are called pseudopodia (sü-də-pō'-dē-ə) *Pseudo* is Greek and means "false" and *podia* means "feet." So pseudopodia are "false feet."

Pseudopodia

In a microscope, the movement of an amoeba along the surface of a glass slide looks something like this:

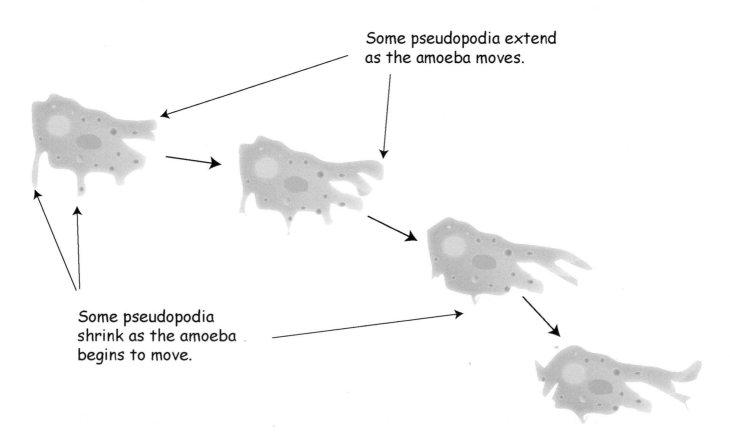

Some pseudopodia extend as the amoeba moves.

Some pseudopodia shrink as the amoeba begins to move.

6.4 Summary

Here are the main points to remember from this chapter:

° Protists are microscopic, one-celled organisms that have both plant-like and animal-like qualities.

° A microscope is a special instrument that makes very small things appear larger.

° There are three main types of protists that are classified primarily on how they move: ciliates, flagellates, and amoebas.

° Ciliates move with tiny hair-like projections called cilia.

° Flagellates move with one or two long whip-like structures called flagella.

° Amoebas move by crawling with pseudopodia, or "false feet."

Chapter 7 Protists II

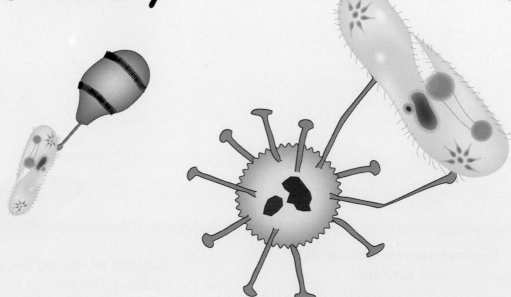

7.1 Nutrition

Because most protists are single-celled organisms, they do not have the advantage of using tissues and organs to process food. Instead, they must gather food, digest nutrients, and eliminate wastes all within a single cell. As a result, protists are much more complicated than cells of other eukaryotic organisms.

7.2 How euglena eat

Some protists contain chloroplasts and use the sun's energy to make food by photosynthesis, just like plants. *Euglena viridis* is one example. Euglena are found in freshwater streams and ponds. Sometimes they are so numerous that the water turns greenish from them.

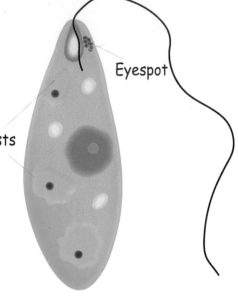

Euglena viridis

Because euglena depend on photosynthesis for food, it is important for them to tell the sunny areas from the shady areas in a pond or stream. To detect light, euglena have a small red spot toward the end of their body near the flagellum. This spot is called the eyespot or stigma. The stigma is actually a shallow cup that detects sunlight only from a particular direction. When the euglena is traveling toward the light, a small part in the base of the stigma is illuminated. When the euglena swims away from the light, the spot is no longer illuminated, and the euglena knows that it is no longer in the path of the sunlight. Using the stigma, the euglena can find the sunlight needed for photosynthesis.

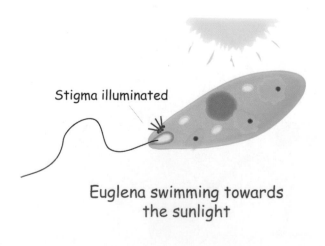

Euglena swimming towards
the sunlight

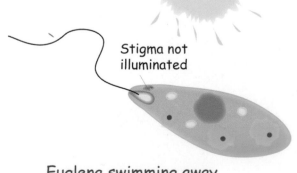

Euglena swimming away
from the sunlight

7.3 How paramecia eat

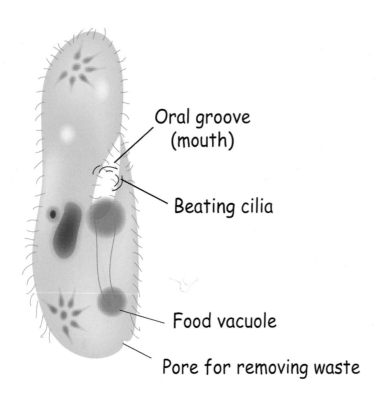

Oral groove
(mouth)

Beating cilia

Food vacuole

Pore for removing waste

Paramecium

Other protists do not have the ability to make their own food through photosynthesis. They need to eat, just like we do. Paramecia, for example, live on bacteria, algae, and other small organisms. They have an oral groove that acts just like a big mouth. They gather their food by rapidly beating the cilia near the oral groove and creating water currents that sweep the food into the opening. The food travels into a food vacuole (va'-kyə-wōl), which is like a tiny stomach for the paramecium. Once food is inside, the vacuole circulates around the cell as the food is being digested. Any undigested food left in the food vacuole is ejected through a small pore.

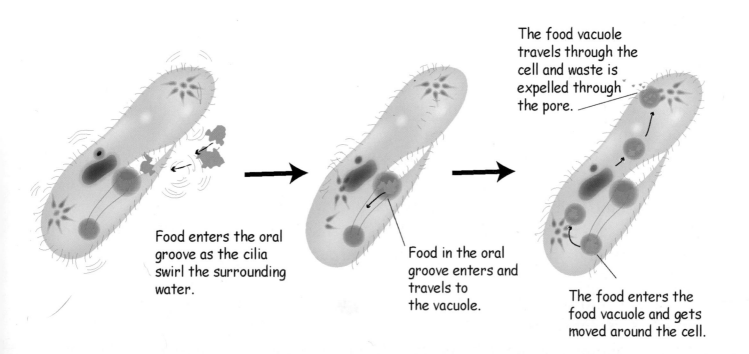

Food enters the oral groove as the cilia swirl the surrounding water.

Food in the oral groove enters and travels to the vacuole.

The food vacuole travels through the cell and waste is expelled through the pore.

The food enters the food vacuole and gets moved around the cell.

7.4 How amoebas eat

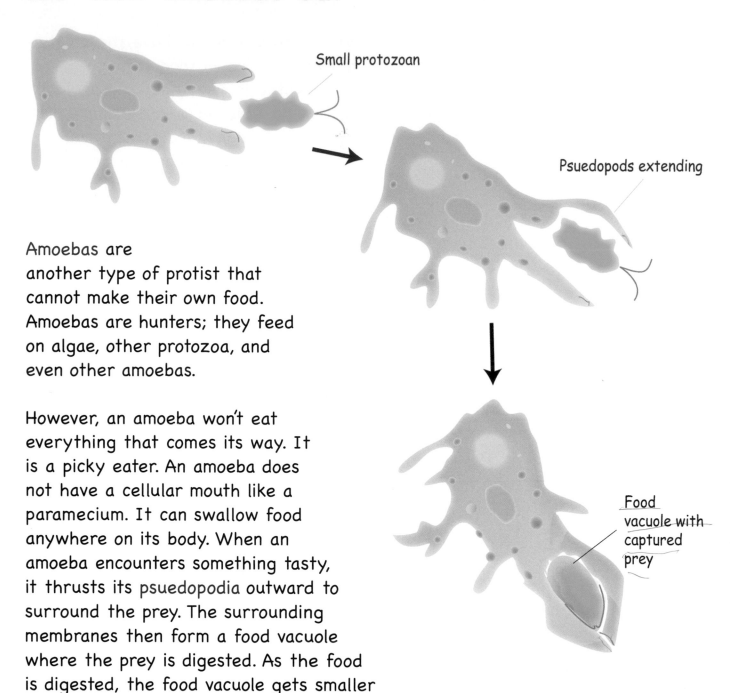

Small protozoan

Psuedopods extending

Food vacuole with captured prey

Amoebas are another type of protist that cannot make their own food. Amoebas are hunters; they feed on algae, other protozoa, and even other amoebas.

However, an amoeba won't eat everything that comes its way. It is a picky eater. An amoeba does not have a cellular mouth like a paramecium. It can swallow food anywhere on its body. When an amoeba encounters something tasty, it thrusts its psuedopodia outward to surround the prey. The surrounding membranes then form a food vacuole where the prey is digested. As the food is digested, the food vacuole gets smaller in size as the nutrients are passed into the cytoplasm (sī'-tə-pla-zəm). Once all of the food has been digested, the food vacuole shrinks and the waste is eliminated through the body surface.

The process of eating of food by surrounding it, used by both the paramecia and the amoebas, is called phagocytosis (fa-gə-sə-tō'-səs). *Phago* comes from the Greek word "phagein" which means "to eat," so a phagocyte (fa'-gə-sīt) is "a cell that eats."

7.5 How other protozoa eat

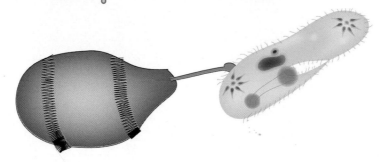

Didinium

There are still other protists that use entirely different methods for capturing and consuming food. Didinium (dī-di'-nē-əm) for example has a single small tentacle which it uses to pierce its prey before swallowing it whole. Podophrya (pō-də-frī'-yə), on the other hand, have many tentacles with knobbed ends. They attach the tentacles to their prey and suck out the insides.

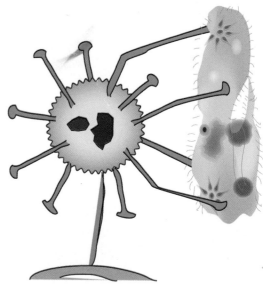

All protozoa are truly remarkable creatures that accomplish an amazing variety of tasks, all within a single cell!

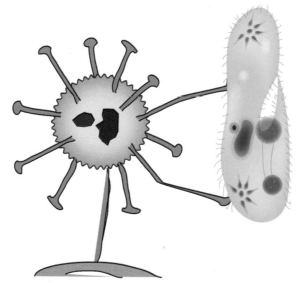

Podophrya

7.6 Summary

Here are the main points to remember from this chapter:

° Euglena, like plants, use the sun's energy to make food.

° Paramecia, amoebas, Didinium, and Podophrya capture other organisms for food by using cilia, pseudopods, or tentacles.

Chapter 8 The Butterfly Life Cycle

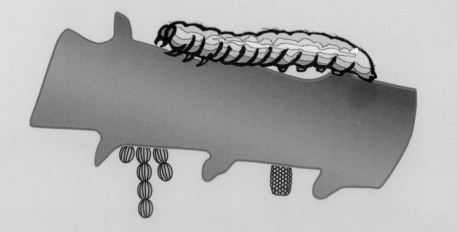

8.1 Introduction

Butterflies are in the order Lepidoptera (le-pə-däp'-tə-rə). *Lepido-* is Greek and means "scales" or "husk" and *-ptera* comes from the Greek word *pteron* which means "a wing." So, the insects in the order Lepidoptera are those that have "wings with scales." This includes both butterflies and moths because they both have similar types of wings.

The life cycle of a butterfly has four different stages: I. eggs; II. egg to caterpillar; III. caterpillar to chrysalis (kri'-sə-ləs); and IV. chrysalis to butterfly.

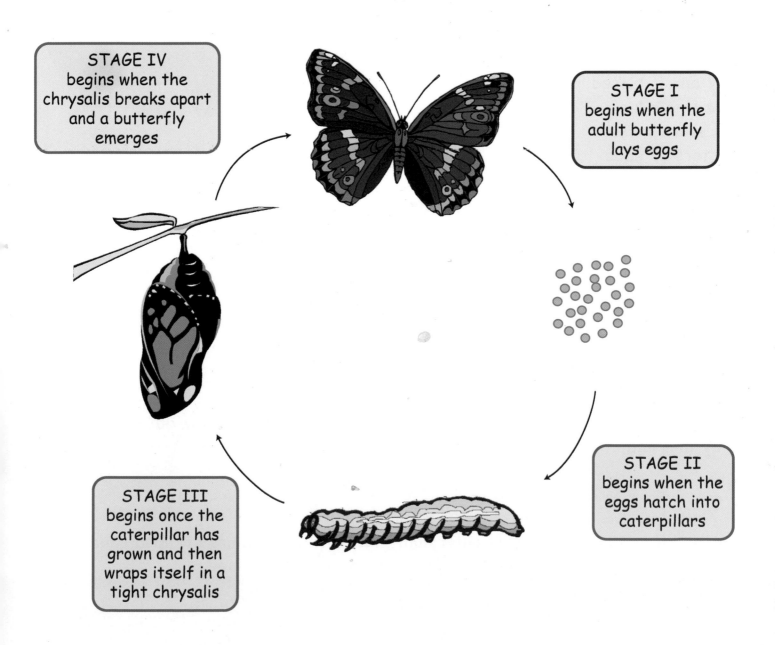

STAGE IV
begins when the chrysalis breaks apart and a butterfly emerges

STAGE I
begins when the adult butterfly lays eggs

STAGE II
begins when the eggs hatch into caterpillars

STAGE III
begins once the caterpillar has grown and then wraps itself in a tight chrysalis

8.2 Stage I: the egg

Butterfly eggs come in a variety of shapes and colors. Some eggs are round, some are barrel shaped, and some look like cheese! They may be decorated with a variety of ridges or raised lines. Also, butterfly eggs are many different colors. Some are brown, blue, red, or green.

All of the eggs are very, very small and are often difficult to see with the naked eye. They can be attached anywhere, from the underside of a leaf to the side of branch. Often, only one is placed on a single leaf, but sometimes clusters of eggs are laid. The monarch butterfly, for example, lays only a single egg on a leaf but can lay over 400 eggs altogether!

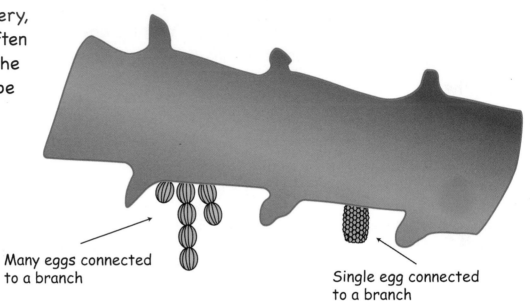

Many eggs connected to a branch

Single egg connected to a branch

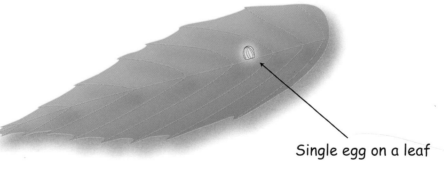

Single egg on a leaf

The little eggs are very tough. They are not washed off by rain or blown away by the wind. A few days after they are laid, the eggs hatch.

8.3 Stage II: the caterpillar

When the egg hatches, a tiny caterpillar emerges. Caterpillars are also called larvae (lär'-vē), and this second stage is called the larval stage.

Caterpillars have long, worm-like bodies. Their bodies are often smooth, but some are very hairy. Many have spines or horns. Some are only brown or green, but many are brightly colored. For example, the monarch caterpillar has bright white, yellow, and black stripes and a smooth body.

When the tiny caterpillar comes out of its egg, it is very hungry. It will first eat the egg from which it was hatched. Then, it will eat the leaf that it is on, and later other leaves. The caterpillar eats and eats and eats.

All day long and all night it keeps eating, pausing only for a little while to rest. As the caterpillar eats, it grows. But the "skin" of a caterpillar does not grow. How does the caterpillar keep growing without its skin growing? The caterpillar sheds its skin as it grows. This is called molting. The caterpillar will molt several times, shedding its old skin, before it is finally ready to become a butterfly. When it is ready to become a butterfly, the caterpillar finds a nice place to hang and spin a chrysalis.

8.4 Stage III: the chrysalis

After a few weeks to many months of eating, the caterpillar is ready to become a butterfly. First, the caterpillar attaches itself to the underside of a stone or twig with a small "button" of silk. (See photo 1 next page.) Before making the chrysalis, the caterpillar wriggles hard to make sure the chrysalis will stay attached. It then begins to wrap itself in a blanket of silk. (See photos 2-3 next page.) When the caterpillar is completely covered, the result is a cozy chrysalis.

Because the caterpillar looks like a tiny doll wrapped in a blanket, the chrysalis is also called a pupa (pyoo'-pə) which is the Latin word for "doll." This stage in the development of butterflies is called the pupal stage.

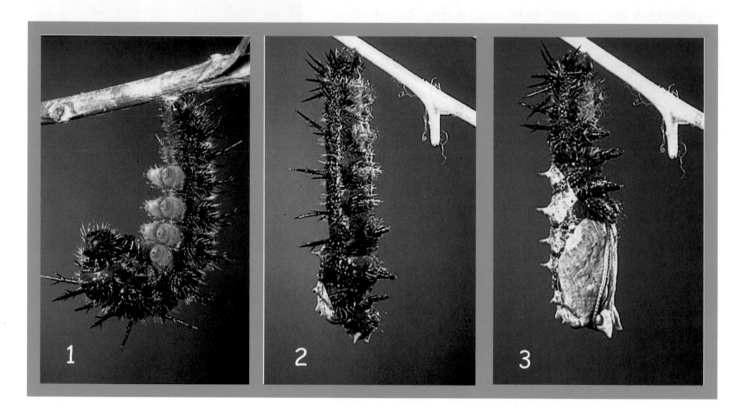

The chrysalis houses the newly forming butterfly. The body of the caterpillar changes dramatically during this time. This change is called a metamorphosis (me-tə-mȯr'-fə-səs). Metamorphosis means *to change shape or form.* Caterpillars change their form from a caterpillar to a butterfly.

In many cases the chrysalis is brown, but in a few species it is brightly colored. The chrysalis for the monarch butterfly is a brilliant green with golden studs along the top. In some cases the chrysalis begins to change color as the butterfly develops. While some butterflies remain in the chrysalis for only a few weeks before emerging, others may stay through the winter months, tightly wrapped in their cozy home.

8.5 Stage IV: the butterfly

When the time comes, the newly formed butterfly begins to emerge from the chrysalis. The covering of the chrysalis splits apart, and the young butterfly crawls out.

The fully developed insect is technically called the imago (i-mä'-gō). *Imago* is Latin and means "an image." The young butterfly cannot fly yet and has difficulty dragging its long body out of the torn chrysalis. Its wings are crumpled up, but soon the butterfly pumps fluid from its swollen body into the wrinkled wings. Once the wings are stretched out, the butterfly begins to fan them as more fluid is pumped from its body into the wings. When the wings are full sized, the butterfly is ready for flight.

Many butterflies are brightly colored with elaborate patterns. For example, the Australian Birdwing butterfly is a brilliant green and yellow. The colors and patterns are made by tiny flat scales that cover the wings. There are tens of thousands of these tiny scales, and the scales overlap each other like shingles on a roof. If you handle a butterfly, the tiny scales can come off and look like powder on your skin. If a butterfly is handled too much, too many scales will come off, and then it won't be able to fly.

The butterfly is now ready to drink the nectar of flowers, lay new eggs, and begin the cycle again. The metamorphosis of caterpillar to butterfly is a truly remarkable accomplishment for such a tiny creature.

8.6 Summary

Here are the main points of this chapter:

○ The butterfly develops from an egg to a caterpillar which then changes into a butterfly. It is an animal that undergoes metamorphosis.

○ Butterflies have wings with many different colors and patterns that are made by thousands of tiny, colored scales.

Chapter 9 The Frog Life Cycle

9.1 Introduction

Frogs are in the kingdom Animalia and in the class Amphibia (am-fi'-bē-ə). *Amphi* comes from the Greek word "both" and *bios* means "life," so amphibia means "both lives." An amphibian is an animal that lives "both lives," one in water and the other on land.

Below is the life cycle of a typical frog. The frog begins life in the water as an egg from which a tadpole emerges and then develops into a frog. The frog leaves the water and spends most of its adult life on land.

9.2 Stage I: the egg

Most frogs live their adult lives on land, but they begin their lives in the water. The first stage in the life cycle of a typical frog is the egg. Adult female frogs lay large quantities of eggs in a moist place like a stream or a pond. This is called spawning. Male frogs then fertilize the eggs.

Frog eggs do not have a shell like chicken eggs, but are covered with a thick jelly-like substance. The jelly-like coating helps protect the inside yolk of the eggs. Because it is not a hard shell, the eggs must be laid somewhere wet or they will dry out. Suitable places include ponds and streams, moist soil, and rotting wood. The jelly-like coating is usually sticky, so the eggs stay together in clumps or strings and stick to stems or the undersides of leaves in the water. This helps keep the eggs from being carried away by currents.

Inside is the yolk of the egg

Jelly-like coating

Frog eggs

9.3 Stage II: the tadpole

Once the eggs have been fertilized, they begin to divide and eventually develop into free-swimming tadpoles. Some tadpoles can be quite large, like the harlequin frog, *Pseudis paradoxa,* which is almost a foot long! Others tadpoles are small, like the Mexican Hylid which is much less than an inch long. Tadpoles do not have jaws, lungs, or eyelids. They have a tail for swimming and gills for breathing under water. They look a little like a fish.

Tadpole

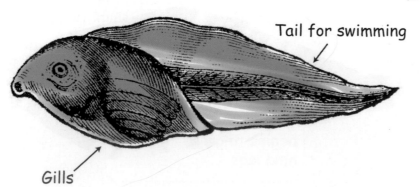

Tail for swimming

Gills

9.4 Stage III: from tadpole to frog

In the next stage, the tadpole begins to change into a frog. This process is called metamorphosis. Remember that metamorphosis means to "change form or shape." A tadpole *changes shape*, starting from a creature that looks like a fish and changing into a frog.

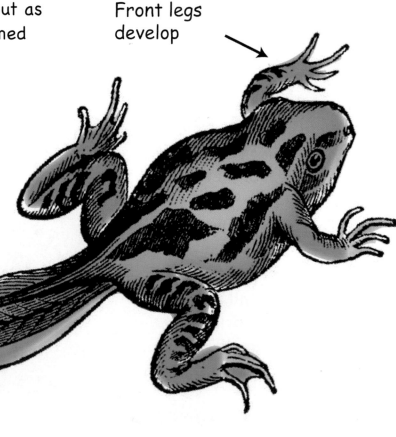

Hind legs begin to develop

The first change to occur is the appearance of hind legs. The hind legs appear as small buds, which then develop into legs complete with toes and webbing. Soon after the hind legs appear, the front legs emerge. The front legs do not come out as buds like the hind legs, but fully formed from beneath the skin. When the front legs emerge, the tail begins to shrink and is taken back into the body of the frog. The mouth changes shape. In certain species, a jaw develops with teeth. The gills disappear and lungs are formed.

Front legs develop

9.5 Stage IV: the adult frog

After the tail shrinks and the lungs develop, the young frog moves onto the land. An adult frog looks very different from a tadpole. The tail is gone and front and hind legs have appeared. The gills are gone and the frog uses lungs to breathe. The eyes have changed shape and have eyelids. The frog now has an "ear" called the tympanic (tim-pa'-nik) membrane which is a small, flat disk that vibrates when there is sound. Jaws have developed, and in some species, teeth have formed. The skin is smooth and has many glands that secrete mucus. This helps keep the frog's skin moist. Most frogs also have a long, sticky tongue to catch flying insects.

Adult frog

Eye

Ear
(tympanic membrane)

Front legs

Hind legs

Frogs come in many different sizes and colors. The smallest frog is the Cuban *Sminthillus limbatus* which is no more than 1.5 inches long as an adult. The largest frog can be found in Africa and is called *Conraua goliath*. It is almost a foot long! Not all frogs are green. Some are brilliantly colored. For example, the Azure Dart Frog is a striking bright blue.

Azure Dart Frog

9.6 Summary

Here are the main points to remember from this chapter:

○ Frogs are called amphibians because they live both in the water and on land.

○ The frog's life cycle goes from egg to tadpole to frog.

○ The process of changing from a tadpole to a frog is called metamorphosis.

Chapter 10 Our Balanced World

10.1 Introduction

The Earth is unique among all of the
planets in our solar system. It is the only
planet that contains life. To this day, life on
other planets has not been found. Also, of
all the planets in our solar system, Earth
is the only planet that provides the right
environment for living creatures. The Earth
is a delicately balanced globe that provides
just the right amount of heat, oxygen, and
other things needed to sustain life.

10.2 Ecosystems

The Earth is an ecosystem (ē'-kō-sis-təm). *Eco-* comes from the Greek word *oikos,*
which means "house." An ecosystem is a community of plants, animals, bacteria,
and other living things *housed* together. With the exception of an outside source
of light (the sun), the Earth's ecosystem is completely closed. This means that
within the Earth's atmosphere,
everything that is needed
for life to thrive can be
found. Nothing else is
needed!

The Earth is a big ecosystem with many plants and animals living together. Smaller ecosystems within the Earth's ecosystem can also be observed. In general, an ecosystem is any balanced environment where food, water, and air are *cycled*. A cycle is simply a series of events that repeats itself.

10.3 The food cycle

Plants, animals, bacteria, and other living things rely on each other for food. Plants provide food for small and some large animals; and some larger animals, like tigers, eat smaller animals. In turn, when animals die, they provide food for smaller organisms, like bacteria and fungi. Bacteria and fungi produce the nitrogen that plants use to make their own food—which takes us back to plants. This is a food cycle. Food for all living creatures is provided by other living creatures. Without this balance, it would be impossible for living things to survive in our ecosystem, the Earth.

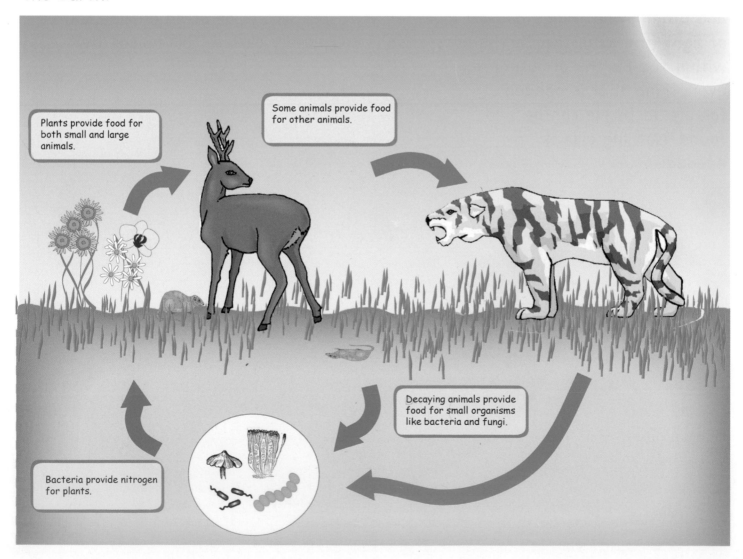

Plants provide food for both small and large animals.

Some animals provide food for other animals.

Decaying animals provide food for small organisms like bacteria and fungi.

Bacteria provide nitrogen for plants.

10.4 The air cycle

The air that we, and other living things, need in order to live is also part of a cycle. Plants use carbon dioxide (CO_2) to make food. In exchange, plants release O_2, oxygen, into the air that we breathe. We then exhale CO_2 which plants use to make food, and so on. If we didn't have plants, we would not have enough oxygen to keep us alive. Plants are a very important part of the ecosystem.

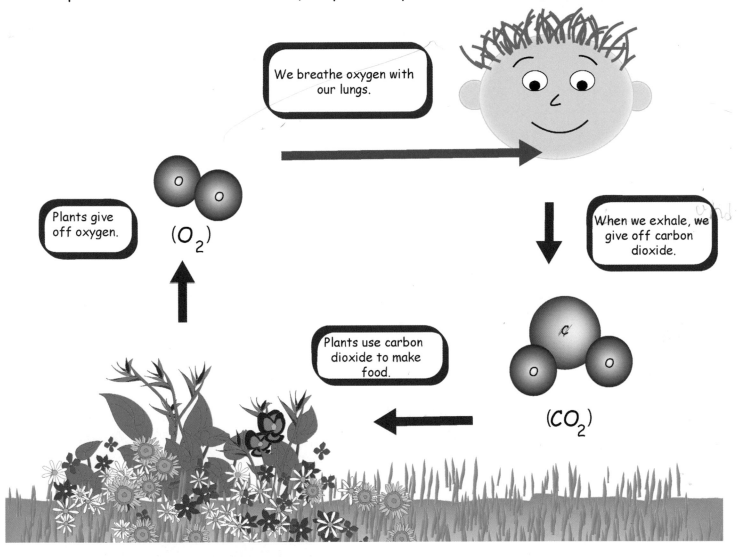

We breathe oxygen with our lungs.

Plants give off oxygen.

(O_2)

When we exhale, we give off carbon dioxide.

Plants use carbon dioxide to make food.

(CO_2)

10.5 The water cycle

There are other cycles in our ecosystem that are very important for keeping everything balanced. Water, for example, gets moved from place to place in streams and rivers and also in the form of rain. The rivers and streams move water from the land to the ocean. Clouds over the ocean pick up the water and move it back onto the land in the form of rain. In this way, rain is cycled throughout the surface of the planet so that plants and animals have enough water to stay alive.

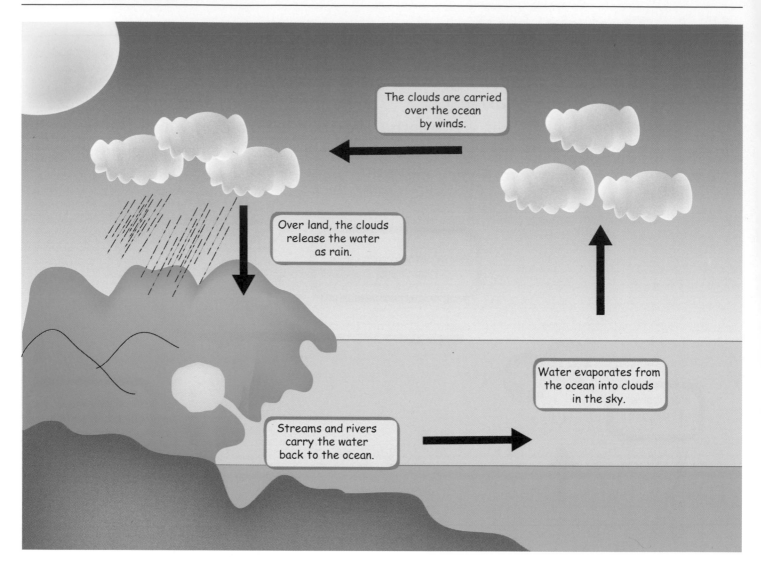

All of these cycles, working together, help keep our ecosystem balanced. Without rain, plants would not get the water they need to grow. Without plants, many animals could not survive. Without animals, smaller organisms would not have the food they need to live. Without the small organisms that make nitrogen, plants would not get all of the nutrients they need and could not provide food for animals.

10.6   Summary

Here are the most important points to remember from this chapter:

- Our world is a delicately balanced ecosystem.

- Many different cycles, like the food, air, and water cycles, contribute to making the Earth balanced, so that living creatures can grow and reproduce.

Glossary - Index

algae (al'-jē) ● an organism that, like plants, uses photosynthesis to make food, 23-24

amoeba (ə-mē'-bə) ● a type of single-celled protist that uses pseudopodia to crawl along surfaces and to eat, 6, 42-44, 48, 49

Amphibia (am-fi'-bē-ə) ● the class under the phylum Mammalia that contains organisms that live part of their life in the water and part on land, 7, 57

amphibian (am-fi'-bē-ən) ● [Gr., *Amphi*, both; Gr., *bios*, life] a creature with "both lives;" frogs and other creatures that live both in the water and on land, 57, 61

Anabaena (a-nə-bē'-nə) ● member of the cyanobacteria, 24

Animalia (ä-nə-māl'-yə) ● the kingdom in which all animals are grouped. An animal is determined mainly by cell type; animal cells have organelles and no cell wall, 5, 7, 57

Arthropoda (är-thrə-pō'-də)● "jointed feet." The phylum under the kingdom Animalia that includes the insects, 7

atom (a' təm) ● [Gr., *atomos*] fundamental unit of matter composed of protons, neutrons, and electrons, 11

bacteria (bak-tir'-ē-ə) ● single-celled organisms that have a prokaryotic cell structure, 14, 24, 36

biology (bī-ä'-lə-jē) ● [Gr., *bios*, life; Gr., *logo*, description] the field of science concerned with describing living things, 2

Canidae (kan'-i-dī) ● the family that includes all dogs, 7

Canis familiaris (ka'-nis fə-mil-ē-ā'-ris) ● domesticated dog, 8

carbon dioxide (kär'-bən dī-äk'-sīd) (CO_2) ● a molecule made of one carbon atom and two oxygen atoms; used by plants to make food, 21-22, 65

Carnivora (kär-ni'-və-rə) ● the order under the class Mammalia which includes meat-eating creatures, 7

carpel (kar'-pəl) ● a tall stem in the center of a flower that collects pollen, 30

caterpillar ● the larval stage of a butterfly or moth, 51-55

cell ● basic building block of life, 4, 11

cell wall ● rigid coat of armor that protects plant cells and prokaryotic cells, 15-18

chlorophyll (klôr'-ə-fil) ● a molecule inside a chloroplast that absorbs the sun's energy for photosynthesis, 21-22

chloroplast (klôr'-ə-plast) ● a tiny organelle inside a plant cell that converts the sun's energy to food, 16-18, 21, 22, 29

Chordata (kȯr-dā'-tə) ● a phylum under the kingdom Animalia that includes all animals that have a backbone, 7

chrysalis (kri'-sə-ləs) ● the silk casing surrounding the caterpillar as it changes to a butterfly or moth, 51, 53-54

cilia (si'-lē-ə) ● small hair-like projections that help some protozoa swim, 42, 44

ciliates (si'-lē-āts) ● a group in the kingdom Protista that uses small hair-like projections to swim, 42, 44

class ● in taxonomy, a subgroup that divides a phylum, 7, 9

conifer (kä'-nə-fər) ● [L., *conus*, cone; L., *ferre*, to carry] an evergreen tree that carries cones and has needles, 23

cotyledon (kä-tə-lē'-dən) ● the area inside a seed that surrounds the embryo and provides food for it, 34-35

cyanobacteria (sī-an-ə-bak-tir'-ē-ə) ● a prokaryotic cell that uses photosynthesis to make food; once called "blue-green algae," 24

cycle ● a series of events that repeats itself, 37, 51, 57, 64-66

Panthera leo (pan-thē'-rə lē'-ō) • the taxonomic name for a lion, 8

Panthera tigris (pan-thē'-rə tī'-gris) • the taxonomic name for a tiger, 8

paramecium (pa-rə-mē'-sē-əm) (*plural* paramecia) • protozoa in the ciliate group, 42, 47, 49

peroxisome (per-äks'-ə-sōm) • an organelle that gets rid of toxins, 16, 17, 18

phagocyte (fa'-gə-sīt) • a cell that eats by surrounding its food, 48

phagocytosis (fa-gə-sə-tō'-səs) • [Gr., *phago*, to eat; Gr., *cyto*, cell] the process of eating by surrounding the food; used by paramecia and amoeba, 48

phloem (flō'-əm) • the tissue in the stem and roots of a plant that carries the food made by photosynthesis downward, 29

photosynthesis (fō-tō-sin'-thə-sis) • [Gr., *photos*, light; Gr., *synthesis*, to make] to make with light; the process by which plants make food, 21, 24, 29

phylum (fī'-ləm) (*plural* phyla) • in taxonomy, a subgroup that is a division of a kingdom, 7, 9

pili (pī'-lī) • long threads on a prokaryotic cell that help the cell stick to surfaces and other cells, 15

pith • central core of a plant; stores food and water, 29

Plantae (plan'-tī) • the kingdom in which all true plants are grouped. A plant is determined mainly by its cell type. All plants have plant cells, 3, 5

plasma membrane (plaz'-mə mem'-brān) • a thin, soft, and greasy film that surrounds all cells, 15-17

Podophrya (pō-də-frī'-yə) • a type of protozoan that uses tentacles to catch prey and remove their insides, 49

pollen (pä'-lən) • in a flower, small grains that carry DNA; found on the ends of stamens, 30, 37

pores • small tunnels that go through the walls of cells and allow molecules to go in and out of the cells, 13

prokaryote (prō-ka'-rē-ōt) • [Gr., *pro*, before; Gr., *karyon*, kernel] a cell that does not contain a nuclear "sack" to hold the DNA. All bacteria are prokaryotes, 14, 15, 19, 24

protein (prō'-tēn) • a large molecule made of many amino acids that is found in the cell and performs special tasks, such as moving molecules from place to place or cutting or repairing molecules, 13, 16, 18

Protista (prō-tē'-stə) • the kingdom that includes mostly microscopic organisms that have both plant-like and animal-like cells. This group includes amoeba, paramecia, and euglena, 3, 6, 40-49

protozoan (prō-tə-zō'-ən) (*plural* protozoa) • a microscopic organism; see Protista, 40

pseudopod (sü'-də-pod) (*plural* pseudopodia [sü-də-pō'-dē-ə]) • [Gr., *pseudo*, false; Gr., *podia*, feet] an extension of the membrane of an amoeba that is used for movement and food gathering, 43, 44, 48, 49

pupa (pyoo'-pə) • the caterpillar wrapped in a chrysalis; pupa is the Latin word for "doll," 54

reproduce (rē-prə-düs') • when living things make new living things of the same kind, 30

ribosome (rī'-bə-sōm) • a sophisticated protein machine that makes other proteins. Ribosomes attach to the rough endoplasmic reticulum, 16, 18

root system • see roots

roots • the part of a plant that lives below the soil and is used for anchoring the plant and absorbing water and minerals, 27-29, 31

rough endoplasmic reticulum (en-də-plas'-mic rə-tic'-yoo-lum) • the place inside eukaryotic cells where proteins are made, 16, 17, 18

sample (sam'-pəl) • in science, the item being studied, 41

kingdom ● the largest grouping of living things; the most commonly used kingdoms are Monera, Protista, Plantae, Fungi, and Animalia, 3-7, 9

larva (lär'-və), (*plural* larvae [lär'-vē]) ● for insects, the stage that occurs when the organism hatches from an egg; the caterpillar, 52

leaf (*plural* leaves) ● the part of a plant that collects sunlight and uses it to make food, 22-24, 27, 29, 31

Leeuwenhoek (lā'-vən-huk), Anton van ● invented a powerful microscope that allowed protozoa ("animalcules") to be seen, 41

Lepidoptera (le-pə-däp'-tə-rə) ● [Gr., *lepido*, scales; Gr., *pteron*, wing] the order that includes insects such as butterflies and moths; both have scales on their wings, 51

Linnaeus (lin-ē'-əs), Carolus ● Swedish physician who began organizing living things into groups. He is considered the founder of taxonomy, 3

lysosome (lī'-sə-sōm) ● organelle inside both plant and animal cells where big molecules are digested, 17, 18

macroscopic (ma-krə-skä'-pik) ● large enough to be seen by the eyes, 23

Mammalia (mə-māl'-yə) ● a class under the phylum Chordata; includes animals that nurse their young and have mammary glands, 7

membrane (mem'-brān) ● a thin layer, 15

metamorphosis (me-tə-mòr'-fə-səs) ● the process of changing shape or changing form, 54, 55, 59, 61

microscope ● an instrument that magnifies very small objects so they can be seen, 41

microscopic (mī-krə-skä'-pik) ● too small to be seen without using a microscope, 23

microtubules (mī-krō-tü'-byülz) ● long protein tubes used by other proteins to move throughout a cell, 17, 18

mineral (mi'-nə-rəl) ● a nutrient that plants obtain from the soil, 28-29, 36, 38

mitochondria (mī-tə-kän'-drē-ə) ● small organelles in eukaryotic cells that make energy, 17, 18

molecule ● two or more atoms hooked together, 11

molt (mōlt) ● for a caterpillar, the process of shedding its old skin, 53

Monera (mə-nē'-rə) ● the kingdom that includes single-celled organisms such as bacteria, 3, 6, 14

mucus (myoo'-kəs) ● a sticky, slippery substance that animals produce, 60

nucleic acids (nü-klā'-ik a'-sədz) ● molecules, such as DNA, that are found inside cells and that give signals to the cell to tell it when to grow and when to make food, 13

nucleoid (nü'-klē-oid) ● the region inside a prokaryotic cell where the DNA is located, 15

nucleolus (nü-klē-ō'-ləs) ● the organelle where parts of the ribosome are made, 17, 18

nucleus (nü'-klē-əs) ● the "sack" inside eukaryotic cells that holds the DNA, 14-18

oral groove ● the opening used as a "mouth" by a paramecium, 47

orders ● in taxonomy, the subgroups that divide the classes, 7, 9

organ (or'-gən) ● many tissues put together to form a particular structure that serves a special function in a living thing; muscles and the liver are examples of organs, 11, 27

organelle (or-gə-nel') ● little "organs" that perform certain tasks inside cells, 16, 18, 21

organism (or'-gə-ni-zəm) ● a living creature, 11

ovary (ō'-və-rē) ● in a plant, the base of the flower where the eggs are kept, 30, 37

oxygen (äk'-si-jən) (O_2) ● a molecule found in the air, 22, 65

Pronunciation Key

a	add	ī	ice	p	pit	ə	a in above	
ā	race	j	joy	r	run		e in sicken	
ä	palm	k	cool	s	sea		i in possible	
â(r)	air	l	love	sh	sure		o in melon	
b	bat	m	move	t	take		u in circus	
ch	check	n	nice	u	up			
d	dog	ng	sing	ü	sue			
e	end	o	odd	yoo	few			
ē	tree	ō	open	v	vase			
f	fit	ô	jaw	w	way			
g	go	oi	oil	y	yarn			
h	hope	oo	pool	z	zebra			
i	it							